T.S. CHERRY

Answers

Collection of Short Books

First published by Tiil Books 2020

Copyright © 2020 by T.S. Cherry

All rights reserved. No part of this publication may be reproduced, stored or transmitted in any form or by any means, electronic, mechanical, photocopying, recording, scanning, or otherwise without written permission from the publisher. It is illegal to copy this book, post it to a website, or distribute it by any other means without permission.

T.S. Cherry asserts the moral right to be identified as the author of this work.

First edition

This book was professionally typeset on Reedsy. Find out more at reedsy.com

Contents

I   WHY ARE YOU PERSECUTING ME?

WHY PRESUME?	3
LOOK BEYOND YOU!	7
WHY ARE YOU PERSECUTING YOUR SALVATION?	10

II   Higher Law & Lower Law

INTRODUCTION	17
LAWS AT PLAY	20
THE LAW OF CAIN	23
THE SEPARATION	27
THE LAW OF ADAM	32
THE LAW OF CHRIST	37

Also by T.S. Cherry   39

I

WHY ARE YOU PERSECUTING ME?

BREAK YOUR PRESUMPTIONS!
Are you one of those who will accept a thing to be of God ONLY if He manifests Himself in the same way, and does things the same way He's always done it?
Do you pray and fast for solution to a problem in your life, but when the solution arrives, you kill it because it doesn't fit in your mold?
Now think about these:
You may know God in a textbook, but not know Him when He shows up in your life;
You know the Bible inside out, but you know it so well that you won't even gi

1

WHY PRESUME?

*And his disciples asked him, saying, Master, **who did sin, this man, or his parents**, that he was born blind?*
   John 9:2

The story of the man born blind is one of the most familiar stories of Scripture. I'd love to take a good look at this story in relation to our disposition on certain life events and occurrences.

While Jesus was passing by, He saw this man who was blind from birth. His disciples wanted to know the real story behind the situation. So, knowing that their Master Jesus knew everything, they asked Him, "Who sinned? Is it this man or his parents?" In essence, their question bordered on whose sin was responsible for the blind man's calamity.

It was a universal opinion among the Jews that calamities of all kinds were the effects of sin. The case, however, of this man was that of one that was blind from his birth, and it was a question which the disciples could not determine whether it was his fault or that of his parents.

"Jesus answered, Neither hath this man sinned, nor his parents: but that the

works of God should be made manifest in him."
John 9:3

But think about it for a moment, why are the disciples asking Jesus if the calamity of this blind man was a result of his sin? Are they saying that this man would have sinned before he was born? Can a new born baby have a past?

Well, it is said that one of the doctrines of the Pharisees and many of the Jews, which appeared in their creed and writings, was "The doctrine of the transmigration of souls." This doctrine presupposed that the souls of men were sent into other bodies for the punishment of some sin which they had committed in a pre-existent state. It was also a doctrine with many, that the crime of the parent might be the cause of deformity in the child.

This seems to have been the foundation of the disciples' question to the Lord Jesus: "Did this man sin in a pre-existent state, that he is punished in this body with blindness? Or, did his parents commit some sin, for which they are thus plagued in their offspring?"

Basically, there was a presumption about this man's blind condition, and it stemmed from the belief around them. So, the man was either blind because of his own sin or that of his parents.

The reality is that this 'presumption mentality' didn't end with that era; it continues today. People tend to believe that something is going wrong around them because they have done wrong in some way. If they don't think this way themselves, others think it for them. But it's not necessarily so.

Let me use a simple analogy about our teams - my husband and I - to make things a bit clearer here.

Every year, my spouse and I go at odds, because even though we're in the same house, we don't root for the same football team. My team, of course, is Dallas Cowboys - Go Dallas - and it's a family team. Everyone in my family that was born and raised up under my dad's roof roots for Dallas.

My spouse, on the other hand, roots for the opposing team. And that opposing team, of course, is the Redskins. So he's a die hard Redskins' fan. Equally, his entire family supports the Redskins every year.

There are several games where we play each other and the reality of it is that we know one of us is going to lose. So, that means I'm either rooting for the losing team or I am rooting for the winning team.

Now, if my team wins or loses, it never really solves the problem of, 'Was I right in supporting the Redskins or Dallas, or was I wrong?"I simply won or lost the game. As a matter of fact, every win doesn't mean I am right in supporting my team, and every loss doesn't necessarily mean that I am wrong either.

Now think about it: How many times have you thought that the reason why something didn't work in your life is because it wasn't meant to be?

"I didn't get the job because God didn't want me to have the job."

"The relationship didn't work because God didn't want the relationship to work."

"My business failed because I didn't do something right."

So, the idea is, "I must have SINNED. I must have done something wrong. God must not be with me, because if He was, I wouldn't be that blind-sighted by what happened."

Listen beloved! Sometimes it's not that you are right or wrong. Sometimes God wants you to be blind. He doesn't want you to know what's happening. He doesn't want you to know what's going on. Yes, He wants to keep you in the dark. He wants to keep you from understanding, or keep you from realizing what is really happening, so He can get the credit.

Think about what Jesus said about the blind man's situation: *"Neither hath this man sinned, nor his parents: but that the works of God should be made manifest in him"* (John 9:3).

Note this: If you can see it coming, you would prepare for it. But if you can't see it coming, you don't know it is God and God alone that is working on your behalf. You don't really know what is happening but when the moment is right, He's going to remove the blinders so you can see the beginning from the end of your situation.

So, why make all manner of presumptions about your situation when God might actually be at work?

It is my prayer, that as you read through this book, God will open your eyes to reality, and that He will change the way you see things.

It is my prayer that God will give you better wisdom, better revelation, and better understanding, so that you can become a better business person, better husband, better father, and in fact, better everything.

2

LOOK BEYOND YOU!

*And as Jesus passed by, he saw a man **which was blind from his birth.*** **John 9:1**

It seems to be very clear from Scripture that everyone knew this man to have been born blind.

To be blind from birth means more than a congenital situation; it means to be blind from the beginning of a situation. So, God is actually saying that there's a situation in your life of which you haven't seen correctly.

The implication is, you don't have a vision concerning that situation. You can't see God in it and you don't have God's Word over your life concerning it. In other words, you are completely blind: you are oblivious to what's going on. And if you are completely blind, then everything you think you know is wrong.

This can best be described as the Damascus Road Experience for you. You know the story. Paul was on a mission to persecute the Christians when he got blinded by a strong light from Heaven. I submit that this was the second time he was blind.

First, Paul was blind from birth. He was blind from the beginning about who the Christians were. After all, Christianity - as far as he was concerned - was a cult, but he was wrong.

He simply didn't see or understand the truth about who the Christians were. He thought they were trying to overtake something that had been in place for several thousands of years. He thought they were going against tradition.

You know, you had to be wrong if you were going against tradition. You had to be wrong if you were going against everything you knew to be right.

So the Christians had to be wrong; right?

Perhaps not!

Second, Paul was blind about what God wanted him to do concerning the Christians. He was blind about his role in that situation. He basically thought his role was to destroy the Christians. Instead of destruction, however, what God really wanted him to do, was to help lead the Christians.

There is no bigger movement that Christians or Christianity had than when Paul changed sides. Just as much as he went after the Christians, with that energy he also went on a mission to make things right. And often times, it is the guilt of our actions that propels us. It is the guilt of knowing that we were wrong that propels us to want to do more.

Think for a moment about who Paul was. He was not just a Johnny come lately. He was not like the rest of the disciples. He was highly educated. He was knowledgeable in the Word of God. He knew what was right. If anyone should have gotten this right, it should have been Paul. But he was so caught up in the tradition of what was right that he didn't give God room to change anything. He didn't give God room to manifest in his situation.

That's what happens to most of us.

Yes, we know the Bible inside out, but we know it so well that we won't even give God a chance to handle things. But you have to understand that, you may know the Word of God, yet not know how that Word applies to your current situation. You may be applying a Word that's not relevant. That is what Paul was doing. He was applying an old Word to a new revelation, a new situation. And the reality is, it didn't fit.

So Saul, who would later be converted to Paul, was breathing threats here and there. He wanted to murder the disciples of the Lord all the way up, until he realized – perhaps, just like most of us in our ignorance - that he had been killing Christ.

You see, we pray and fast for solutions to our problems. But when the solutions arrive, we kill them because we refuse to look at them in a new light. We kill the anointing that we have been praying and fasting for because it's not in our own mold. We will only accept God if He comes the same way, and does things the same way He's always done it.

Beloved, it's time to lift up your eyes and look beyond you!

3

WHY ARE YOU PERSECUTING YOUR SALVATION?

And I fell unto the ground, and heard a voice saying unto me, Saul, Saul, why persecutest thou me?And I answered, Who art thou, Lord? And he said unto me, I am Jesus of Nazareth, whom thou persecutest. **Acts 22:7-8**

There is a strong necessity in getting converted, even as believers. This isn't about conversion from sin but from being an enemy of God by attacking what God has blessed. Jesus says it best, *"Saul, Saul, why are you persecuting me?"*

Saul made a profound statement here: "Who are You, Lord?" That is to say, "I don't even know You on a personal level. I don't know Your voice, Lord."

You see, you may know God in a textbook, but not know Him when He shows up in your life!

By implication, Saul didn't recognize the Lord in his situation. The Lord said, *"I am Jesus the Nazarene, the one you are persecuting"* (Acts 22:8, NLT). In other words, "I am the anointing. I am all you've been waiting on. I am the One sent to you."

"You have been crying out and praying, and I answered you. But when I did, you persecuted the answer I sent to you. You killed the very people I sent to you. You destroyed and broke down the very people I sent; people you were supposed to help."

You see, Saul was supposed to help or assist the Christians, but he was busy hurting them instead. So, sometimes we think we're persecuting people, ideas, concepts, and businesses for God, but what we're really doing is persecuting God and His plans.

That is like supporting the wrong team. Now, imagine that I go purchasing things - socks, jersey and everything else – from the RedSkins. Then the Dallas team comes over to find out if I would get a jersey, and I say, "Rebuke you; I don't even know You. Don't ask me for any money. Don't ask me for any support. I don't support you all because I don't recognize who's side you're on."

I made an assumption and my assumption was wrong.

I want you to think of it as the heavens and the earth playing a game; only that the stakes are much higher here. When earth wins, you don't get blessed - the people lose their livelihood, and you lose positions and territories that the Lord meant for you to have. When earth wins, people suffer, the holocaust is born in the hearts of men, and all men become miserable.

If you look at our surrounding, you can see how miserable everyone seems to be. For some reason, it's because they're playing for the wrong team. And no matter how right you think you are, the Spirit is grieved because the Spirit knows you just made points for earth when you're supposed to be playing for heaven.

So, when I look at your score board today and what you've done, earth has four points but heaven has zero.

I want you to think about that!

Think back at your actions all day long. How many actions scored points for heaven and how many actions scored points for your flesh - the earth. How many things did you do out of your flesh and how many did you do out of the Spirit of God? How many things did you do just to protect yourself?

So, are you sure that you're playing for the right team?

You could be playing for heaven or you could be blind-sighted from birth, needing God to restore your vision. Think about the positions you hold in your life, if you're blind. God could be waiting on you to be converted about your co-workers, about your loved one, about a job opportunity, about that situation which you are so busy being right!

You might have destroyed people, opportunities, relationships, business ideas, partnerships, all because you were blind. But now God wants to give you something you have never had before, and that is His perspective on the situation.

The truth is that no one wants to be the blind man playing on the wrong team because they score points, make touch downs and support the wrong team.

You know, every morning you commit to playing for Team Heaven. But the score points for Team Earth seems to be getting higher and higher all because you're blind. You don't know who to throw the ball to. You don't know who's on your side and who's against you; who's right and who's wrong. You're just playing with everything you have. You're putting your whole heart, soul and everything you have.

But you're killing Christians. You're killing the anointing. You are constantly attacking God, and God wants to know from you, "Why are you persecuting Me? Why are you attacking Me? Why are you destroying what I am trying to do in the earth?"

God is saying, "You're killing Me. And like Saul, you're doing it all in My Name. You're destroying My plans and you're saying, "I'm destroying it for God; I'm doing God's work." You are using My work to hurt My people.

"You think you're doing God's work, but you're really destroying the blessings that I keep sending you. Every time I try to bless you, you attack and destroy the people I send to you, all because they don't fit in your idea, in your box, your old ways of understanding.

"I don't fit in your theology, and you don't get to cage Me. My ideas and concepts are far beyond what you could possibly understand. You don't know Me. You just think you do. And like Saul, you can be busy being the smartest person in the room. Yet you can be wrong nonetheless, by destroying everything I'm trying to build and doing it all in My Name.

Every time I send people into your life, I want you to take them to the next level, but you attack them, instead."

WHOSE SIDE ARE YOU ON

The question now is who's side are you on - heaven's or earth's?

Look over your life; are there some things you attack or reject? Have you sought God on the matter?

You could have formed an opinion that from the very beginning was wrong. You might have the wrong idea about that person, that co-worker or that business.

Perhaps you thought a person, a business or company was a blessing from God, but you see, the opposite can also be true. If you did not seek God on the matter, you could be wrong.

You might need to be converted in your thinking and believe system, so that you could see the truth about the business, the relationship, and even your family.

What God is saying in essence is, "Stop attacking Me and My people, and all My opportunities that I keep sending in your life because of your blindness." Like Saul, God wants to knock you off your high horse and let you know that you are actually fighting Him.

I know you don't think of this often, but have you ever thought of the fact that you could be the person God is speaking about? You could be the enemy of God because you are busy scoring points for the wrong team. You could be persecuting and destroying God's work, His people, His moves while you think you're working for Him.

ANSWERS

It's important you realize that sometimes you are saying that what is right is right and what is wrong is wrong. But then, there are times when you think you're making the right decisions when actually you're making the wrong decisions. And many times, the people you think are good could be bad and the people you think are bad could be good. The truth is, there's a bit of evil in the best of us, and there is some good in the worst of us.

The question remains, who's side are you on?

II

Higher Law & Lower Law

WALK IN GOD'S PLANS FOR YOUR LIFE...DAILY!

Higher Laws, Lower Laws – A Deeper Understanding of Law and Grace *is meant to help you re-evaluate your relationship with God and progress in life based on higher and lower laws - Divine or Supernatural laws - which are capable of establishing your life firmly in the plans and purposes of God.*

God designed your life almost like a partnership between you and Him. So, He is available both in the best and critical moments of your life.

4

INTRODUCTION

God is a Father like no other!

I can't help but think about the fact that when it comes to God, I don't need anyone else's permission to be accepted before Him. People don't necessarily have to like or approve of me, for Him to do same. No!

Often times, God blesses people who the world wouldn't necessarily approve of. And I like that because it gives me hope that when I do wrong – knowingly or unknowingly - I can still present myself before God. And when I'm right, I can still come to Him. The good thing is, as the songwriter says, He is always there beside me. He is always there to catch my fall. He is always there no matter what my situation appears to be – good or bad.

You know, these days, its commonplace to hear people describe 'the glass' either as half-full or half-empty. The general idea is that 'the glass' describes our perspective of events, situations or circumstances in life. It implies that if you think the glass is half-full, you have chosen to look at your situation from a positive perspective. Conversely, if you see the glass as half-empty, you have decided to look at things from a negative point of view.

This analogy, however, is not really an accurate way to portray philosophy. The truth is, the glass is neither half-empty nor half-full; it's not half anything! Believe it or not, it is completely filled. Whether it is filled with water and air or water only, matter completely occupies every space.

This understanding is important because it'll help you view life from a balanced perspective. What do I mean by this? There should be an element of 'God at play' in the situations of your life. God must be found in the midst of the happenings in your life – whether good or bad. God designed your life almost like a partnership between you and Him. So, He is available both in the best and critical moments of your life.

Many times, we don't sense this partnership because we don't give it the deserved attention. So we find that we are moving on all alone, making our decisions and only come to discuss them with God later on. The reality is, when we do that, we waste time, energy, and effort. Why? Because God has already laid out His plans for us! Rather than waste the time He has given us, we could simply follow His plans.

This book is meant to help you re-evaluate your relationship with God and progress in life based on higher and lower laws - Divine or supernatural laws - which are capable of establishing your life firmly in the plans and purposes of God.

INTRODUCTION

T. S CHERRY

5

LAWS AT PLAY

And when Peter was come down out of the ship, he walked on the water, to go to Jesus. But when he saw the wind boisterous, he was afraid; and beginning to sink, he cried, saying, Lord, save me.
Matthew 14:29-30

For so many things in life, there are laws at play. And the average person knows that laws are connected to consequence in a way. For example, you are bound to obey certain laws while driving on the road.

Nevertheless, the reality is that, even when there's punishment attached to not obeying the law, all laws do not necessarily attract some form of punishment. Some laws are in play naturally, whether you realize it or not. Take for instance, the Law of Gravity. It is not a law that attracts punishment.

The Law of Gravity simply states that what goes up must come down. It keeps your feet to the ground. But the same thing that keeps your feet to the ground can also limit you. For example, if you need to be able to rise above a situation, you are grounded because the Law of Gravity is at work.

In order to go higher, you need to find a higher law that counteracts gravity. And that can only be the Law of Aerodynamics. This law counteracts the Law of Gravity and allows you to fly above your situation. This is the law that allows airplanes to stay in the air. So, even though gravity is still at play in keeping everything to the ground, an airplane is able to stay afloat in the air because of a higher law.

Now, the problem is, if you don't know there's the higher Law of Aerodynamics, for instance, you can be grounded by the Law of Gravity for as long as possible. If you look at this from a Biblical perspective, you can see the same idea at play in the Law of Walking on Water.

Matthew 14:27-30 says, *"But straightway Jesus spake unto them, saying, Be of good cheer; it is I; be not afraid. And Peter answered him and said, Lord, if it be thou, bid me come unto thee on the water. And he said, Come. And when Peter was come down out of the ship, he walked on the water, to go to Jesus. But when he saw the wind boisterous, he was afraid; and beginning to sink, he cried, saying, Lord, save me."*

Notice from the Scriptures that as long as Peter stayed focused, he was able to walk above his situation. But once he focused on his situation instead of God, he actually went down. When we look at that, we are again able to see two laws at play – the law of fear and that of faith. It seemed natural to be afraid of the storm. But there was a higher law that could defy the fear of the storm and cause a man to walk on water.

When Peter kept his focus on God, he activated the higher law that could keep him above the storm and make him walk on water as on plain ground. This higher law would continue to be in force only if he was able to keep his focus on God. However, at the point that he wasn't able to keep his focus on God anymore, the lower law brought him down and he began to sink.

That's an important lesson.

In essence then, 'this glass' that we describe as either half-full or half-empty represents our lives. It is supposed to be half-full of living water and for some of us, half-full of laws that we may not even believe in. But you know that believing or not believing in a law changes nothing.

For instance, I may decide that I don't believe in gravity. That doesn't really stop gravity from being in effect. I'm still walking on the ground; I'm not floating in the air. Gravity is still activated in my life, whether I understand it or not.

In the same way, there are laws at play in life whether you realize them or not. And until you implement a higher law, you could just be struggling under the effects of these laws. I'll discuss a few of these laws in the chapters that follow.

6

THE LAW OF CAIN

And He said, "What have you done? The voice of your brother's blood cries out to Me from the ground." **Genesis 4:10, NKJV**

The Law of Cain is at work in many people's lives, even when they don't seem to realize it. It's a law that is basically activated by our decisions, choices and eventual actions.

When Cain killed his brother Abel, God confronted him with the fact that Abel's blood was crying to Him from the ground. So, practically the Law of Cain turns a person's living into blood that cries out from the ground for justice. It means there's death in such a life, because we understand that blood signifies death. When Moses turned the waters of Egypt into blood, we understand that he actually brought death into the situation of that nation.

Most people describe justice in terms of 'Karma,' which is not necessarily a word in Christian circles; nevertheless, it is well understood by many. Karma is just another word that means someone brought a curse upon himself based on his life choices. This is exactly what happened to Cain. He walked himself into a curse by his choice of actions.

Genesis 4:11-12 (NLT) says, *"Now you are cursed and banished from the ground, which has swallowed your brother's blood. No longer will the ground yield good crops for you, no matter how hard you work! From now on you will be a homeless wanderer on the earth."*

What came on Cain was a direct consequence of what he chose to do.

This curse, however, did not stop at Cain but went down through his lineage. The time came that Cain's grandson, Lamech, did exactly what his grandfather did. Genesis 4:23-24 says, *"One day Lamech said to his wives, "Adah and Zillah, hear my voice; listen to me, you wives of Lamech. I have killed a man who attacked me, a young man who wounded me. If someone who kills Cain is punished seven times, then the one who kills me will be punished seventy-seven times!"*

Lamech said he destroyed a young man for wounding or hurting him. Now, a young man implies that he was an innocent man who did not mean to willingly hurt Lamech. Yes, he probably hit Lamech or caused him pain, but Lamech responded by killing him. The Amplified Bible puts Lamech's confession of his crime in better perspective: *"for I have slain a man [merely] for wounding me, and a young man [only] for striking and bruising me"* (Genesis 4:23, AMP). Did you see that?

It became clear that there was a curse on this family. Lamech found himself doing exactly what his grandfather had done. And he said, *"If someone who kills Cain is punished seven times, then the one who kills me will be punished seventy-seven times!"*

We should be careful about retaliation because sometimes we may be retaliating against people who are innocent. You thought they were guilty, but they were innocent, and in retaliating against them you bring yourself under the Law of Cain.

And remember, it doesn't stop with you. You also bring your seed - which can be your kids, your company, and anything else you produce in the future - under the same curse. And it's basically because you decided to avenge yourself.

When you tip the scales in the wrong direction, you pay a price. When that happens, you think it is God punishing you, but no, you walked yourself under a law that is already in effect.

Like I said earlier, gravity doesn't punish you; it's already in effect. In the same way, the Law of Cain isn't designed to punish you; it's designed to make sure there is balance in the world. This means that essentially, you punish yourself by your choices.

A good example of this is what happened to Israel during their journey to the Promised Land. The 23rd chapter of the Book of Numbers explains how Barak brought a prophet called Balaam to bring a curse on the children of Israel, but it was practically fruitless. In the end, Balaam advised that the only way of getting the people cursed is to get them to curse themselves.

Balaam knew that there was a law already in place: he couldn't curse what God had blessed. But he knew there was a higher law, which was the Law of Balance. So, he could only cause the people to curse themselves by breaking laws that pre-existed. Don't forget that Moses had told them, *"These laws are not mere words – they are your life!"* (Dueteronomy 32:47) So, when the Israelites broke the laws that preserved them, they automatically walked themselves into the curse.

Now, if you are aware of these pre-existent laws, you can avoid breaking them. But if you are not aware of them, you could bring yourself, your descendants, your company, etc., under the consequences of breaking them, and you may not even realize it, because it's not something that is necessarily common knowledge. It's not something that is talked about a lot. It's not something that a lot of people believe in. But that doesn't change its impact.

Your treatment of others directly affects your success in life. That's why you should let the Lord fight your battles. Think about it, if you're trying to fight back and the person wasn't trying to hurt you originally, the ground will cry out. That is, you will bring yourself under the effect of a law that works against those who fight or hurt the innocent.

7

THE SEPARATION

But of the tree of the knowledge of good and evil, thou shalt not eat of it: for in the day that thou eatest thereof thou shalt surely die. Genesis 2:17

A lot of people wonder why Abel had died but his blood was still crying to God from the ground. We need to know that this is not just the physical kind of death we know. This is the death of separation. It's like what happened in the Garden of Eden when God said, *"But of the tree of the knowledge of good and evil, thou shalt not eat of it: for in the day that thou eatest thereof thou shalt surely die"* (Genesis 2:17).

Adam and Eve didn't die right that minute they ate the fruit, but there was a separation from God that caused death in their lives. This is the death that Cain also experienced. Cain had to separate from his people, his tribe, and go alone. But we know he did not completely go alone, because the Bible tells us he took a wife.

ANSWERS

Nevertheless, he still had to go alone, separate from the other tribes.

So, we see the overall picture of separation being the consequence of breaking the law. This separation could also be from what was rightfully theirs. It could be the separation from a blessing. It could be a separation from interacting with other people. And that's why even parents should be careful when they separate and try to break up marriages.

You should be careful when you try to break up a relationship. In fact, you have to be extremely careful and be certain that the situation is not ordained by God. If it is ordained by God, you might be putting yourself in real trouble.

Listen, not every marriage is ordained by God. Equally, every situation is not ordained by God. But if it is, you must honor it. For instance, if God put someone in a position and you did whatever you could to get them fired or put out of that position, then you could come into a curse because that position was given to them by God. It was a blessing given to them by God, and you separated them from that blessing. In doing that you brought a curse upon yourself.

Think about it, how many times have you done someone wrong? How many times have you done shady businesses? How many times have you cheated someone to make a profit? How many times do you think someone doesn't deserve something? How many times do you think someone else has hurt or wronged you?

How many times do you think someone needs to be punished

when in reality the person is innocent? Just because you feel that way doesn't mean you're right, and doesn't mean that God is on your side. That something happened does not mean that you are right in hurting someone else. You could be wrong and then being wrong, you could essentially destroy yourself.

Is it really worth giving up your success just to get back at someone and hurt them? Is it really worth destroying your future just so you can feel good that someone who hurt you gets punished or hurt too? Is it really worth it? Yes, you may get a temporary gratification, but in the long run, you are actually killing yourself. You are introducing death into all that concerns you.

Death is a major separation from reality: you are separated from happiness; you are separated from love; you're separated from abundant life; you are separated from success; you are separated from blessings; and you are separated from peace.

This is why people who appear to be very, very successful get to a certain place and they're unhappy; some of them even commit suicide. Yes, you got to your destination, and yes, you had the appearance of great success, but that success may not be blessed if you didn't do it right.

If you didn't get there the right way, such success cannot be blessed. If you climbed over people to get there or hurt people all along the way, it cannot be blessed. Yes, you got what you wanted, but be careful because you may not want what you get.

Furthermore, how you end things is very important too. How you come off of a job or end a relationship, for instance, is important, perhaps even more than how you started. Let's say you want to quit your job, how you handle things is extremely important. Be careful that you don't hurt people on your way out of relationships just because you don't want to be with them anymore.

Don't create tension just because you don't need that business relationship anymore. The reality is, you'll pay for it. If you are wrong and the people cry out to God for justice, it definitely puts you under the Law of Cain, whether you believe in it or not.

THE CURSE OF WANDERING

Another way the Bible describes the curse on Cain's life is that of a wanderer. Genesis 4:11-12 (NLT) says, *"Now you are cursed and banished from the ground, which has swallowed your brother's blood. No longer will the ground yield good crops for you, no matter how hard you work! From now on you will be a homeless wanderer on the earth."*

A second thing to note is that the Law of Cain introduces a spirit of wandering. This wandering depicts the fact you are unsettled. You have trouble sitting still or staying in a place. So you see, it is a spirit, and this spirit won't let you make roots or build something; it makes you to keep moving.

Have you ever met a con man? I think almost everyone has. You'd notice a con man has to keep conning people. He never seems to get ahead. He cons someone and takes three steps forward, but in effect, he takes six steps backward. So, he always needs to con people over and over and over again.

If you ever paid attention to the life of people who were cons, say 10 years ago, and then 10 years later, you'd notice they haven't really gotten anywhere. In addition, they have this negative outlook on life, because so many voices of blood from the ground are crying out against them. They have been drinking blood, and it changes their perspective of life. You know, they're actually drinking death. So, they constantly see the negative side of life.

Their life is a direct consequence of the Law of Cain, so they live as wanderers moving back and forth without any meaningful progress.

It is possible that I can bless someone like that and give them good things but they can destroy and mess them all up by bringing themselves under the Law of Cain. That's because they cannot see anything positive. They only see the negative, because they're just consumed with blood in their life.

8

THE LAW OF ADAM

And unto Adam he said,... Thou shalt not eat of it: cursed is the ground for thy sake; in sorrow shalt thou eat of it all the days of thy life;
Genesis 3:17

The law of Adam means that a person has position without accompanying power. Such a person is merely a Christian without access to the power of healing, peace, love and grace.

If you live like that, when someone asks how you're doing, you tell a lie. You pretend that you're all right when in actual sense you are not. You say, "I'm blessed," but your life is cursed. You say, "I'm making progress," but you're actually being set back to correct the mistakes you refused to correct in your life.

Your life is repeating same cycles because you have refused to grow. You have refused to do things the right way. You would rather hurt your brother and your sister like Cain did, rather than just simply do what is right so that God can bless you.

So you know the story, Cain and Abel were twins in the eyes of God. In other words, you and the person that you think did you wrong are twins in the eyes of God. Cain saw that Abel was living a sacrificial life because he was a shepherd. Abel was involved in building people up, unlike Cain who merely lived off the seeds that God had given him which he put into the ground to grow.

Cain eventually plots to kill his brother because he thinks his brother's life is somehow happier than his. That's more like what we do today. We decide to hurt someone else because we think they're living a happier life than we are, and that somehow, their happiness is taking away from our happiness.

That isn't the only reason why we hurt people of course, but that's what is in the particular example of Cain and Abel. It's important to understand that the person who you think is beneath you, or has done something wrong, is equivalent to you in the eyes of God.

Notice that when God gave Cain seed to put in the ground to grow, that was His provision, which was meant to feed him. Cain, however, turns around and gives it back to God. In essence, he gave back to God what God gave him. It is like the parable of the talents. Matthew 25:15 says, *"And unto one he gave five talents, to another two, and to another one; to every man according to his several ability; and straightway took his journey."*

After a long time, when the Master - Who of course represents

God in this story - came back, the servants returned to settle their accounts: *"And so he that had received five talents came and brought other five talents, saying, Lord, thou deliveredst unto me five talents: behold, I have gained beside them five talents more. He also that had received two talents came and said, Lord, thou deliveredst unto me two talents: behold, I have gained two other talents beside them. Then he which had received the one talent came and said, Lord, I knew thee that thou art an hard man, reaping where thou hast not sown, and gathering where thou hast not strawed: And I was afraid, and went and hid thy talent in the earth: lo, there thou hast that is thine"* (Matthew 25: 20, 22, 24-25).

To the persons who multiplied their five and two talents respectively, the Master said, *"Well done, good and faithful servant; thou hast been faithful over a few things, I will make thee ruler over many things: enter thou into the joy of thy lord"* (Matthew 25:23). It finally gets down to the fact that the one who had one talent buried it in the ground and it did not profit him.

That's just what Cain did.

Genesis 4:3 says, *"And in process of time it came to pass, that Cain brought of the fruit of the ground an offering unto the LORD."* Cain presented some of his crops as a gift to the Lord. And God seemed to be saying to him, "You did not profit from what I gave you!"

If you are in business, you do understand that profit is what you have after you have paid your employees, settled your mortgage, your family, etc. In other words, it shows that you made the best use of what God put into your hands for effective growth.

To bring God's response to Cain closer, God is basically saying, "I sent you employees but you abused them because you didn't see the value of their contribution.

"You abused the relationships that I sent into your life to bless you.

"You missed opportunity after opportunity because you kept making decisions without Me. Your life didn't profit you.

"At the end of the day, when you look back, you don't have anything left. You didn't make gain; you didn't multiply anything. All you have is what I gave you in the first place. You had just enough to eat, but that's exactly what I gave you."

So, when Cain shows up and gives God what God had given him, God says, *"You're wrong. You didn't make any profit. Where's the profit? You simply paid your employees but made no profit."*

Beloved, what God gives you has to grow. You have to be able to feed other things off of it, not just yourself. For God's sake, you can't just give Him back the food that He gave you.

Abel, on the other hand, was feeding the flocks. In other words, he took the food God gave him and multiplied it by giving it to others - the animals. When it was time to offer to God, he had something that could be laid down for the sacrifice after conscientiously feeding his flock.

I'm sure you can see also why Jesus implored Peter to feed His flock. Three times He called Peter and spoke about this. He stressed on it three times because He knew Peter would deny Him three times.

John 21:15-17 says, *"So when they had dined, Jesus saith to Simon Peter, Simon, son of Jonas, lovest thou me more than these? He saith unto him, Yea, Lord; thou knowest that I love thee. He saith unto him, Feed my lambs. He saith to him again the second time, Simon, son of Jonas, lovest thou me? He saith unto him, Yea, Lord; thou knowest that I love thee. He saith unto him, Feed my sheep. He saith unto him the third time, Simon, son of Jonas, lovest thou me? Peter was grieved because he said unto him the third time, Lovest thou me? And he said unto him, Lord, thou knowest all things; thou knowest that I love thee. Jesus saith unto him, Feed my sheep."*

Cain was supposed to feed the flock with what he was given. But what did he do? He gave God back the food. Why are you giving the food back to God? The truth is, that's not what God wants for your life. He doesn't want you to just survive. And if you are just surviving, you are wrong. You want God to choose your side but God chooses the side of Justice. In Acts 10:34 (NLT) Peter said, "I see very clearly that God shows no favoritism." He doesn't do it.

Now I ask you, "What has God put in your hands?" Grow it. Multiply it. Give it a turnaround until it becomes a blessing to more and more people. Let your position be accompanied by power!

9

THE LAW OF CHRIST

The Law of Christ is the Law of Grace.

Christ shows that there's a higher law at play here – the Law of Grace. He said if He is killed, being innocent, He would be raised back up again in three days.

You need to understand this. Anyone that you think you hurt and or you think you destroyed, God will raise them back up again because they were the ones that were wronged. And this is good news for those of us who've been wronged. You can now see that God is going to raise you up in three days, because this is the Law of Christ; it is stronger than the Law of Abel.

The Law of Christ is God's answer to Abel's cry from the ground. God heard Abel and answered him through Christ. Abel is asking, "How long more before we get justice?" Christ comes with the answer: "You don't have to ask how long anymore. You'll be raised up in three days!" But how long is three days? It is however long it takes you to go from death to resurrection – especially resurrecting yourself in forgiveness.

Christ took care of His forgiveness when He was crucified. He said, *"Father, forgive them, for they don't know what they are doing"* (Luke 23:34, NLT). You need to be raised from the dead. But do you really want to be resurrected? Then you need to be able to say, "Father forgive them because they don't know any better." Forgive them and let it go. They don't know any better.

They hurt you on purpose; yes. But they don't know any better. They think your blessings, your love, and all you have, somehow hurts them. They really think that hurting you will make them feel better. At the end of the day, you still have to let it go. If you don't let it go, you don't get resurrected.

God shows you how to be resurrected. You don't want the Law of Adam at play here. You don't want to be crying out for generations. You want this done in three days: Let it go; cry about it; cry to God about it, forgive them and move on!

You don't have to be going round and round in the world like this. Where necessary, you will have to ask for forgiveness. You will have to apologize where you need to, and forgive where you need to. You're going to cry to God and ask to be freed from whatever curse you've put on yourself. And in three days, you're going to get your life back.

That is where you need to be.

Also by T.S. Cherry

Teach. Torah Relevance. Purpose

T.S. Cherry was encouraged to write her first messianic book due to her health to ensure her teaching could be read by her children: *T.S. Cherry Torah Study Methods*. Writing "You are that Tree" greatly inspired Cherry when she had "little confidence" in her messianic teaching ability. Her second book "Let us Make Man" offers insight into the Seven Heavens; Which are the Kingdom of Heaven.

YOU ARE THAT TREE

An exposé on two trees in the Garden of Eden – the Tree of Life and the Tree of Good and Evil. A journey of self-discovery: From being misplaced to discovering our true identity and pre-ordained path, while learning to remove obstacles in the way of our God-ordained purpose.

LET US MAKE MAN- SERIES

LET US MAKE MAN – an exposé on the Seven Heavens is sequel to T.S Cherry's startling life-changer, You are The Tree! It describes the man who is the tree of life and his journey from the FIRST HEAVEN to the SEVENTH HEAVEN.

FREE Children's Bible Study Lessons
You are that Tree Children: Children's Bible Study and Sunday School Lessons